Brilliant Model Answers

Published by

Educationzone Ltd

London N21 3YA
United Kingdom

British Library Cataloguing in Publication Data:

A catalogue record for this publication is available from the British Library.

978-1-906468-13-2

Email us for further information:

info@psychologyzone.co.uk

For more information:
Visit our website for exam questions and answers, teaching resources, books and much more:
www.psychologyzone.co.uk

Content for Model Answers

Please note: this book is not endorsed by or affiliated to the AQA exam board.

Important information

! *Do not skip this page!*

◼ Isn't the exam supposed to be unpredictable?

This guide is part of Psychologyzone's *Brilliant Model Answers* series covering A-level Psychology. Use it alongside the Psychologyzone series Brilliant Exam Notes to get the best out of your learning.

This guide to the 'Issues and Debates' topic provides a full set of exam-style questions and model answers to help you do well in the exam. After all, your Psychology exam is based on answering questions – what better than to have a book that already has the answers for you?

The exam board has deliberately developed the A-level Psychology specification so that the questions are to some extent 'unpredictable' in order to discourage students from attempting to rote-learn (memorise answers) using pre-prepared questions. This makes it difficult to predict what's going to be asked.

We have tried to make the unpredictable 'predictable'.

There are over 60 model answers in this book. We have covered most of the different types of question they can ask you for each topic on the specification. You can adapt the model answers provided to most types of questions set in the exam.

◼ Some of your model answers seem very long. Why?

Some of the answers are much longer responses than you would need to write in the exam to get top marks. **This is deliberate.** We have written them this way to enable you to have a better understanding of the theories, concepts, studies, and so on. If you do not write as much as we have, don't panic! You don't need all of the content to achieve a good grade.

As you may be using this as a study book, we thought we'd write the model answers in a way that means you can also revise from them, so we sometimes expand on explanations or give an example to help you understand a topic better.

Many of the model answers start by repeating the question; in the real exam you don't need to waste time doing this – just get stuck in!

Remember: in your exam, your answers will be marked according to how well you demonstrate the set assessment objectives (AOs). We have tried to provide model responses that show you how to meet these AOs. Each example provides you with 'indicative content' – in other words, the response gives you an idea of points you could make to achieve maximum marks. It doesn't mean these are points you must make! The purpose of these model answers is to inspire you and demonstrate the standard required to achieve top marks.

Exam skills

How will my answers be assessed?

Your teachers will have explained that your answers in the examination will be assessed on what examiners call **assessment objectives (AO)**. If you can familiarise yourself with these AOs, this will help you write more effective answers and achieve a higher grade in your exam. There are three assessment objectives: **AO1, AO2** and **AO3**.

By now, your teachers should have given you a lot of practice exam questions and techniques for how to answer them. The aim of this book is not to teach you these skills, but to show you how it's done – to model the answers for you.

Just to remind you, below are the AQA assessment objectives:

AO1 Knowledge and understanding

Demonstrate knowledge and understanding of scientific ideas, processes, techniques and procedures.

What does this mean?

The ability to describe psychological theories, concepts, research studies (e.g., aim, procedures, findings and conclusions) and key terms. The exam questions can cover anything that is named on the specification.

Example

Explain the process of synaptic transmission. **[5 marks]**

Outline the role of the somatosensory centre in the brain. **[3 marks]**

AO2 Application

Apply knowledge and understanding of scientific ideas, processes, techniques and procedures:

- in a theoretical context
- in a practical context
- when handling qualitative data
- when handling quantitative data.

What does this mean?

Application questions require you to apply what you have learnt about in Psychology (theories, concepts and studies) to a scenario (situation) often referred to as 'stem' material. A scenario will be a text extract or quote given in the question. You are treated as a psychologist, and you need to explain what is going on in the situation from what you have learnt.

Example

Chris suffered a stroke to the left hemisphere of his brain, damaging Broca's area and the motor cortex. Using your knowledge of the functions of Broca's area and the motor cortex, describe the problems that Chris is likely to experience.   **[4 marks]**

AO2   Evaluation

Analyse, interpret and evaluate scientific information, ideas and evidence, including in relation to issues, to:

- make judgements and reach conclusions

- develop and refine practical design and procedures.

What does this mean?

Evaluation simply means assessing the 'value' (hence 'evaluation') of a theory or study you have been describing. There are many ways you can evaluate theories or studies. For students, evaluation often takes the form of the strengths and weaknesses of the theory and/or study, but evaluation can also be in a form of 'commentary' (neither strength nor weakness but more in the form of an 'analysis', which is still an evaluation).

Example

Outline one strength and one limitation of post-mortem examination.   **[2 marks + 2 marks]**

What are the different types of exam questions?

We have grouped the exam questions into four different types:

Identification questions	Multiple-choice questions, match key words with a definition, tick boxes, or place information in some order or in a box.
Short-response questions	Questions worth up to 6 marks (1, 2, 3, 4, 5 or 6 marks). These are often questions asking you to 'outline', 'explain', or 'evaluate' a theory or a study.
Application questions	These require you to apply the psychological knowledge you have learnt (theories, concepts, and studies) to a real-life scenario given in the exam question.
Long-response question	These questions require longer answers and are worth over 6 marks (8, 12 or 16 marks). The long-response answers found in this book will be mainly for 16 mark questions.

How are the model answers structured?

We have tried to structure your learning by breaking down the model answers into four distinct categories:

Key terms, concepts, and theories that are named on the AQA specification are covered by the identification and short-response questions (e.g. explain what is meant by the term…).

Research questions asking you to outline a study, describe a theory or give an evaluation are covered by short-response questions (e.g. briefly outline one study that has…).

Application questions require you to apply your knowledge to a made-up scenario (situation) and are covered under application questions.

Essay questions 'Outline and evaluate', or 'Discuss'-type questions are covered under long-response questions. Some long-response questions also require the application of knowledge.

Specification: Issues and debates

- Gender and culture in Psychology – universality and bias. Gender bias including androcentrism and alpha and beta bias; cultural bias, including ethnocentrism and cultural relativism.

- Free will and determinism: hard determinism and soft determinism; biological, environmental and psychic determinism. The scientific emphasis on causal explanations.

- The nature-nurture debate: the relative importance of heredity and environment in determining behaviour; the interactionist approach.

- Holism and reductionism: levels of explanation in Psychology. Biological reductionism and environmental (stimulus-response) reductionism.

- Idiographic and nomothetic approaches to psychological investigation.

- Ethical implications of research studies and theory, including reference to social sensitivity.

Gender bias in Psychology

Key terms

Q1 Explain what is meant by 'universality' in psychological research. **[2 marks]**

Universality refers to the applicability of psychological research. This term considers whether a set of findings can be applied to all humans, regardless of gender, culture, or time.

Q2 Explain what is meant by 'bias' in relation to gender. **[2 marks]**

Gender bias refers to instances where men and women are treated or represented differently in psychological research, and the views held may not necessarily be true for that gender. There are two forms of gender bias: alpha and beta. This bias can have both scientific consequences, where psychologists may develop inaccurate views of human behaviour, and social consequences, manifesting in the perpetuation of prejudices and discrimination.

Q3 Explain what is meant by 'androcentrism'. **[3 marks]**

Androcentrism, stemming from the issues of beta bias, is the practice of considering male behaviours as the benchmark. It occurs when female behaviours are compared to an all-male standard. As many female behaviours deviate from established male norms, androcentrism often results in the pathologisation of female behaviour, viewing it as unhealthy or undesirable.

Q4 Explain how 'androcentrism' has affected psychological research. **[3 marks]**.

Androcentrism has significantly influenced psychological research by increasing its social sensitivity. When an androcentric study portrays females as abnormal, it can have broader implications for the female population in society. Furthermore, it tends to perpetuate existing prejudices and socially determined stereotypes within psychological research and the theories derived from it.

Q5 Outline gender bias in psychology, including reference to androcentrism. **[6 marks]**

Gender bias refers to instances where men and women are treated or represented differently in psychological research, the views held may not necessarily reflect the truth for that gender. There are two forms of gender bias: alpha and beta. This can lead to both scientific consequences, where psychologists develop inaccurate views of human behaviour, and social consequences manifesting in the perpetuation of prejudices and discrimination.

Alpha bias involves overstating and exaggerating the differences between male and female. In some cases, it may bolster the position of women positively, but in others, it may also diminish their position, leading society to view them more negatively. For instance, Bowlby's Monotropic Theory can be seen as promoting the mother's attachment to an infant, which is desirable in a custodial setting. Still, it may hinder a woman's ability to return to the workplace as they need to stay home and care for the child.

Beta bias refers to undermining the differences between male and female. It results from a lack of female representation in a given research study and a mistaken assumption that the findings from the same study can be applied to both genders, thus undermining any potential differences in behaviour that the study addresses. Androcentrism stems from beta bias, suggesting that male thinking/behaviour is the norm. This can devalue women, as they often exhibit behaviours outside the male standard, making them appear abnormal or undesirable.

Q6 Explain what is meant by 'alpha bias' and describe one example of psychological research that demonstrates alpha bias. [4 marks]

Alpha Bias involves the exaggeration of differences in behaviour between male and female. In some cases, it may enhance the positive perception of women, but in others, it may diminish their position, leading society to view them more negatively. Bowlby's Monotropic Theory demonstrates alpha bias because it overstates the differences in the importance of women as mothers and males as fathers in attachment formation. This study could be seen as improving the position of women in society's eyes, but conversely, it could also be argued to reinforce the prejudice that women must stay at home to care for their children.

Q7 Explain what is meant by 'beta bias' and describe one example or psychological research that demonstrates beta bias. [4 marks]

Beta bias refers to undermining the differences between male and female due to a lack of female representation in a research study and the mistaken assumption that the findings can be applied to both genders. Research into the fight or flight response, often conducted on male animals, demonstrates beta bias. It was assumed that this response would be the same for both sexes. However, Taylor et al. (2000) found that females adopt a 'tend and befriend' approach to ensure the survival of their offspring.

Q8 In relation to gender bias in psychology, evaluate the role of alpha and beta bias. [6 marks]

One strength of alpha bias in psychological research is that it has contributed to the development of feminist psychology. Feminists argue that while real biological differences exist, it is often socially determined stereotypes that play a more significant role in perceived gender differences. For example, Bowlby's Monotropic theory can be supported not only due to the presence of estrogen in women but also because of the social stereotype that expects women to stay home to care for children while men should work. This is a strength because modern feminist psychologists aim to rectify this exaggerated imbalance in both theories and research by eliminating stereotyping, ultimately reshaping people's perceptions.

A positive consequence of beta bias is that it promotes the view of men and women as equals. This perspective has resulted in equal treatment in legal terms, such as no-fault divorce, parental leave, and equal access to education and employment. However, beta bias can divert attention from power imbalances between genders and the fact that we still live in a male-dominated society. Seemingly neutral actions can inadvertently benefit the dominant group. For example, equal parental leave overlooks the biological demands of pregnancy, childbirth, and breastfeeding, disadvantaging women. While beta bias can have beneficial consequences, it can also perpetuate the misrepresentation of one gender and sustain prejudices in society.

However, while it can be argued that beta bias has constructive benefits, it can also be criticized for downplaying the fact that there are real physiological and psychological differences between men and women. For example, in Bandura's bobo doll study, a consistent finding was that boys were more aggressive than girls, attributed to higher levels of testosterone in boys compared to girls, which is linked to a higher level of aggression. This suggests that by minimizing the differences in male and female behaviour, we may put our children at a disadvantage as we fail to recognize their distinct characteristics, which could significantly impact child-rearing practices.

Application question

Q9 "A psychologist asked men aged 25 to 35 years to keep a diary recording how many miles they walked in a week. The psychologist also asked each man to climb a flight of stairs, then recorded each man's heart rate. For each man, the number of miles walked in the week was correlated with their heart rate after climbing the stairs. The findings showed a significant negative correlation. A national newspaper reported the findings under the headline 'Everyone should walk for a healthy heart'."

(a) Explain how the newspaper headline might be an example of beta bias. **[2 marks]**

The newspaper headline states that 'everyone' should walk for a healthy heart, even though the study's findings suggesting this only involved male participants. As it undermines potential differences between males and females on this matter, it can be defined as an example of beta bias.

(b) Briefly suggest one way in which psychologists might address the problem of beta bias in their research. **[1 mark]**

To address or avoid the issue of beta bias in their research, psychologists should include both male and female participants in their studies.

Essay questions

Discuss gender bias in psychological research. Refer to examples of alpha and beta bias in your answer.   **[16 marks]**

Psychology has long been male-dominated, giving rise to androcentrism, the view that male thinking and behaviour constitute the norm. Consequently, psychological theories often yield a male-centric worldview, potentially resulting in gender bias.

Gender bias occurs when men and women are treated or portrayed differently in psychological research, and the held views may not necessarily reflect the reality of both genders. There are two primary forms of gender bias: alpha and beta, each with distinct consequences. Alpha bias involves theories or research that exaggerates differences between men and women, potentially devaluing one gender. It may bolster the position of one gender positively in some scenarios but can also negatively affect perceptions. For instance, Bowlby's Monotropic Theory assumes that mothers are crucial for a child's attachment and that a lack of maternal care can lead to irreversible emotional and social damage. While this promotes the idea that women should prioritize child-rearing over work, it also suggests that fathers are less important in custodial battles. Furthermore, if Bowlby's theory is incorrect, many fathers are denied the satisfaction of raising their children.

On the other hand, beta bias refers to the practice of downplaying differences between males and females. It often stems from inadequate female representation in research studies and an erroneous assumption that findings can be universally applied to both genders, thus negating any potential differences in behaviour the study might uncover. For example, biological research on the fight-or-flight response has frequently used male animals, assuming that this response is the same for both sexes. However, Taylor et al. (2000) discovered that females adopt a 'tend and befriend' approach to ensure the survival of their offspring.

One strength of gender bias in psychological research is its role in the development of feminist psychology as a response to androcentrism. Feminist psychologists seek to challenge androcentric generalizations, which often pathologize female behaviour as unhealthy or undesirable. They argue that while real biological differences exist, socially determined stereotypes play a more significant role in perceived gender differences. For instance, feminist psychologists highlight that Bowlby's Monotropic Theory can be supported not only due to the presence of estrogen in women but also because of the social stereotype that women should stay home to care for children while men work. This strength lies in the efforts of modern feminist psychologists to rectify these imbalances by removing stereotypes, thereby altering societal perceptions.

Conversely, beta bias has led to societal acknowledgment that men and women are equal, resulting in equitable treatment in legal and educational realms, such as no-fault divorce, parental leave, and equal access to education and employment opportunities. However, beta bias can divert attention from existing power imbalances in our predominantly male-dominated society. Seemingly neutral actions may inadvertently favor the dominant group. For example, advocating for equal parental leave overlooks the unique biological demands of pregnancy, childbirth, and breastfeeding, ultimately disadvantaging women. While beta bias can have positive outcomes, it can also perpetuate gender-based prejudices.

Nonetheless, critiquing beta bias reveals its shortcomings, primarily its failure to acknowledge genuine physiological and psychological differences between men and women. For example, Bandura's bobo doll study consistently found that boys exhibited more aggression than girls, attributed to higher levels of testosterone in boys. Neglecting these differences potentially places children at a disadvantage, as we fail to recognize their distinct characteristics, which could significantly impact child-rearing practices.

Additionally, it is crucial to recognize that gender bias in psychological theories and studies may lead to the discovery of gender differences. However, these differences may arise not from inherent disparities between genders but from biased research methods. For instance, feminists argue that laboratory experiments disadvantage women because controlled lab settings poorly reflect women's real-life experiences. A meta-analysis study by Eagly and Johnson observed that real-life settings judged both genders as more similar in leadership styles than lab experiments did. Moreover, the gender of the researcher can also influence results; Rosenthal found that male experimenters were often more accommodating to female participants, leading to inferior performance by male participants.

Cultural bias in Psychology

Key terms

Q11 Which two of the following are examples of ethnocentrism? **[Total 2 marks]**

Shade two boxes only.

When a Chinese researcher:

- A. assumes findings from research in other countries also apply to people in China.
- B. chooses to carry out research with people from China rather than with people from other countries.
- C. expects people from other countries to behave in the same way as people from China.
- D. thinks that people from China are superior to people from other countries.
- E. treats people from China in the same way that she treats people from other countries.

Q12 Explain what is meant by 'cultural relativism' in psychology. **[3 marks]**

Cultural relativism refers to the notion that norms, values, or even a given set of findings from a research study can only be understood or applied within specific cultural contexts. In essence, it means that these matters cannot be applied to any other culture, except for the one that is under consideration. For example, when defining abnormal behaviour using failure to function adequately, women in Muslim cultures who remain housebound can be seen as maladaptive or irrational behaviour, and it may be indicative of agoraphobia, but in fact, it is differences within cultures that provide a reason for this behaviour.

Q13 Explain what is meant by 'cultural bias' and describe one example or psychological research that demonstrates cultural bias. **[4 marks]**

Cultural bias refers to the practice of overlooking differences between cultures by viewing a particular behaviour from the perspective of the researcher's own culture. Most psychological theories and research techniques have their roots in a Western worldview. When this knowledge is applied to members of other cultures, it reflects a cultural bias. For example, classic social influence studies of conformity by Asch were originally conducted on American participants from an individualistic culture. However, when replicated in collectivistic cultures, they yielded significantly different results. This can be explained by the fact that collectivistic cultures place a greater emphasis on group needs and collective responsibility, which promotes greater conformity, suggesting cultural differences.

Q14 Discuss the role of 'cultural relativism' in psychology.   **[6 marks]**

Cultural relativism refers to the notion that norms, values, or even findings from a research study can only be understood or applied within specific cultural contexts. Essentially, it means that these matters cannot be applied to any other culture except the one under consideration. For example, when defining abnormal behaviour using the criterion of failure to function adequately, women in Muslim cultures who remain housebound might be seen as displaying maladaptive or irrational behaviour. However, these behaviours may be better understood as reflections of cultural differences.

Q15 Suggest two ways in which researchers might reduce cultural bias in their research. **[2 marks]**

Possible ways:

- Do not attempt to extrapolate findings or theories to cultures that are not represented in the research sample.

- Use researchers who are native to, familiar with, or immersed in the culture being investigated.

- Carry out cross-cultural research rather than focusing solely on one culture.

- Avoid assuming universal norms or standards across different cultures.

- Be sensitive to cultural norms and standards when designing research or reporting findings.

- Study a single culture to understand that culture (adopt an emic approach).

- Take a reflexive approach, constantly reflecting on one's biases when conducting research.

Q16 Explain what is meant by ethnocentrism and describe one example or psychological research that demonstrates ethnocentrism.   **[4 marks]**

Ethnocentrism refers to the practice of judging other cultures by the standards of one's own culture. In some cases, it involves a belief that one's own culture is superior to the culture being judged, leading to a view that any behaviours not conforming to the researcher's own cultural norms are deficient.

An example of ethnocentrism in a moderate form is evident in Ainsworth's research involving the Strange Situation technique. Ainsworth assumed that a moderate level of separation anxiety indicated secure attachment. However, this assumption led to misinterpretation when applied outside of American culture. For instance, German mothers were seen as cold and rejecting because of children's apparent indifference upon the mother's absence. In reality, these differences were rooted in distinct child-rearing practices that encouraged independence and interpersonal distance.

Essay questions

Discuss cultural bias in psychology. Refer to two examples of research in your answer.

[16 marks]

Cultural bias refers to the practice of overlooking differences between cultures by viewing behaviour from the perspective of the researcher's own culture. Most psychological theories and research techniques have their roots in a Western worldview. When this knowledge is applied to members of other cultures, it reflects a cultural bias.

For instance, classic social influence studies on conformity by Asch were originally conducted on American participants from an individualistic culture. However, when replicated in collectivistic cultures, the results differed significantly. This can be attributed to collectivistic cultures placing a greater emphasis on group needs and collective responsibility, resulting in higher levels of conformity.

A specific form of cultural bias is ethnocentrism, where researchers judge other cultures by the standards of their own culture. A moderate example of this is seen in Ainsworth's research using the Strange Situation technique. Ainsworth assumed that moderate separation anxiety indicated secure attachment. However, this assumption led to misinterpretations when applied outside of American culture. For instance, German mothers were viewed as cold and rejecting because their children displayed indifference during the mother's absence. This interpretation failed to consider the differences in child-rearing practices that encouraged independence and interpersonal distance.

One positive aspect of cultural bias in psychology is that it has spurred the development of indigenous psychology, leading to different theories in various countries that incorporate cultural differences. For example, Cochrane's study found that African-Caribbean immigrants were seven times more likely to be diagnosed with a mental disorder. However, these rates weren't consistent with rates in Africa, challenging the validity of the Western DSM. This discrepancy led to Afrocentrism, advocating for African-centered psychological theories that dispute the idea that European values universally describe human behaviour.

Nonetheless, it's essential to question whether cultural bias is as prominent today. The individualistic-collectivistic distinction, often used to categorize cultures, may no longer be as applicable in our interconnected world. Takano and Osaka's study found that 14 out of 15 comparisons between the USA and Japan showed no evidence of this distinction, suggesting that cultural bias may be less significant today.

Another strength of cultural bias in psychology is that it has sparked the emic-etic debate. An imposed etic approach emphasizes the uniqueness of each culture by focusing on culturally specific phenomena, reducing cultural bias but limiting generalizability. In contrast, an etic approach seeks universal behaviours and is more prone to cultural bias. Both approaches have their merits, emphasizing the need for a balanced understanding of human behaviour that considers both universal and culture-specific aspects.

Cultural bias has also resulted in unrepresentative findings. Smith and Bond found that 66% of social psychology studies focused on American participants, while 32% studied Europeans, and only 2% represented the rest of the world. Additionally, Sears reported that 82% of studies used undergraduates, further narrowing the demographic represented. This not only limits the generalizability of research globally but also within Western cultures, leading to theories that are imposed ethics and, consequently, a limited understanding of human behaviour.

Free-will and determinism

Key terms

Q18 Which two of the following statements describe a strongly deterministic view? **[2 marks]**

Shade **two** boxes only.

- A. People are always responsible for their own actions
- B. People behave in a random fashion
- C. People's behaviour always has a cause
- D. People exercise full choice over how they behave
- E. People have no choice about how to act

Q19 Explain the free-will and determinism debate. **[3 marks]**

The free-will vs. determinism debate revolves around the attempt to establish which of the two forces has a greater influence on human behaviours. Advocates of free will, such as Maslow, argue that an individual's own volition influences their choices and behaviours. Proponents of determinism, such as B.F. Skinner, argue that choices are influenced more by external forces beyond the control of an individual.

Q20 Outline five types of determinism. **[5 marks]**

Determinism is the belief that an individual's behaviour is influenced or governed by either internal or external factors, rather than being the result of their own free will. There are two main levels of determinism: soft determinism, which suggests that while human behaviour is somewhat constrained, individuals still have the capacity to make conscious choices, and hard determinism, which asserts that our behaviour is invariably dictated by internal or external events beyond our control, rendering free will incompatible with hard determinism. There are also five specific types of determinism:

1. Biological determinism: Behaviour is caused by internal biological influences such as genetics and hormones.
2. Environmental determinism: Behaviour is caused by features of the environment through classical and operant conditioning.
3. Psychic determinism: Behaviour is caused by unconscious conflicts.
4. Cultural determinism: Behaviour is influenced by the culture an individual belongs to.
5. Technological determinism: Behaviour is influenced by advancements in technology and media..

Q21 Using an example, explain what is meant by soft determinism. **[3 marks]**

Soft determinism is a belief that acknowledges that there may be internal/external influences on behaviour beyond an individual's control, but individuals still have the capacity to make their own rational decisions regardless of these forces. An example of this belief lies in the cognitive approach to psychology, which recognizes that choices may be constrained by the limits of an individual's cognitive systems but also acknowledges that individuals can make choices nonetheless.

Q22 Using an example, explain what is meant by hard determinism. **[3 marks]**

Hard determinism, also recognized as fatalism, is the belief that absolutely all choices and behaviours are influenced by internal or external forces beyond the control of an individual. This belief claims that there is no room for individual choices. An example lies in the psychodynamic approach to psychology, specifically psychic determinism, which suggests that all choices are influenced by the authority of the unconscious.

Q23 Briefly explain the concept of biological determinism. **[2 marks]**

Biological determinism is the view that internal biological structures, such as hormones and genetics, influence and control various behaviours. For example, the Biological Approach suggests that OCD is caused by our genetic makeup, supported by findings that people with 1st-degree relatives who suffer from OCD are more likely to also suffer from OCD.

Q24 Briefly explain the concept of environmental determinism. **[2 marks]**

Environmental determinism is the view that previous reinforcement contingencies, other environmental influences of the past, and agents of socialization are factors that both influence and control choices. For example, the Behavioural Approach suggests that phobias are acquired through classical and operant conditioning.

Q25 Briefly explain the concept of psychic determinism. **[2 marks]**

Psychic determinism is the view that the authority of the unconscious and repressed childhood traumas influence and control choices and behaviours. For example, the Psychodynamic Approach suggests that gender behaviours are acquired during the phallic stage of development and through the resolution of the Oedipus/Electra complex, resulting in identification with the same-sex parent.

Q26 With reference to a behaviour, explain the distinction between hard determinism and soft determinism. **[3 marks]**

Hard determinism suggests that any and all behaviours, such as decision making, are influenced or controlled by internal or external forces beyond the control of an individual. Soft determinism acknowledges that internal or external forces that may influence behaviours exist but ultimately lie within an individual's own conscious mental capacity. An example of this distinction can be seen in the obsessions and compulsions of OCD. Hard determinism views these behaviours as solely caused by biological factors, while soft determinism recognizes the possibility of a traumatic experience playing a role in addition to genetic vulnerability, as seen in the diathesis-stress model.

Q27 Briefly give one strength of taking a determinist approach in psychology. **[3 marks]**

One strength of determinism is that it is consistent with the aims of science. The notion that human behaviour is orderly and obeys laws places psychology on equal footing with other more established sciences. In addition, research focused on the prediction and control of human behaviour has led to the development of treatments, therapies, and behavioural interventions that have benefited many individuals. For example, antipsychotic medications like chlorpromazine in the treatment of schizophrenia have a strong association with the dopamine hypothesis. Moreover, the experience of mental disorders like schizophrenia, where individuals experience a total loss of control over their thoughts and behaviour, casts doubt on the concept of free will, as no one would 'choose' to have schizophrenia. Thus, at least in terms of mental disorders, behaviour appears to be determined.

Q28 Briefly give one limitation of taking a determinist approach in psychology. **[3 marks]**

A limitation of accepting a determinist approach in psychology is that the view itself may be harmful to the well-being of individuals. Numerous studies, such as those conducted by Roberts et al., have discovered that individuals with a strong belief in fatalism (a hard determinist stance) are at a greater risk of developing depression later in life. This suggests that determinism as a belief could actually reduce the quality of life for people who accept this view.

Application questions

Q29 Read the item and then answer the questions that follow.

Extract from a newspaper article:

> **Coping with Life's Pressures**
>
> Depression often runs in families, but many depressed people have serious social problems or have experienced traumatic events in the past. However, many people find ways to cope. What we need is the will to overcome our problems.

With reference to the item above, explain what is meant by 'determinism'. Refer to three types of determinism in your answer. **[4 marks]**

The term determinism refers to the view that all choices and behaviours are influenced or controlled by internal/external forces beyond the control of an individual. Although this basic principle is a consensus, the determinism approach still has many divisions regarding what forces exactly control behaviours. Proponents of biological determinism would say that behaviours such as depression are determined by biological constructs such as genetics, as the condition "often runs in families." Those who believe in psychic determinism, on the other hand, would argue that depression is actually a manifestation of repressed memories of 'traumatic events in the past.' Soft determinism would acknowledge all of these factors but would ultimately argue that individuals have the conscious mental capacity to 'overcome these problems' if they desired.

Q30 Jonny is 25 years old. He is a very anxious person. Colleagues tease him at work because he chews his pen all the time and spends hours tidying his desk. He finds it difficult to make friends and has never had a girlfriend.

Use your knowledge of psychic determinism to explain Jonny's behaviour. **[4 marks]**

Jonny's behaviour of being a 'very anxious person' could be explained in terms of a manifestation of repressed childhood traumas that he may have experienced. His behaviour of 'chewing his pen all the time' could also be seen as determined by a fixation, but more specifically, an undersatisfaction that he may have experienced during his oral stage of development. Jonny's behaviour of tidying his desk all of the time could also be seen as being determined by an undersatisfaction during his anal stage of development, and his inability to have a girlfriend could be the result of a failure to resolve the genital stage of development.

Joel has learned to get his own way at school by having fights with other children. His two older brothers were both excluded from school for injuring other children. Recently, Joel has also been excluded from school for attacking another child.

Q31 Determinism is the belief that all choices and behaviours are influenced by internal/external forces beyond the control of an individual. There are varying views within this approach as to what forces exactly determine behaviour. Proponents of biological determinism, for example, would argue that Joel's aggression is the result of constructs such as genetics, given how 'his two older brothers were also excluded from school' due to their aggression, suggesting that the behaviour runs in his family. Advocates of environmental determinism, on the other hand, would claim that Joel's aggression has actually been caused by the influence of positive reinforcement experiences, given how he had learned 'to get his own way at school by having fights.'

Discuss two or more types of determinism. Refer to the case of Dancho as part of your discussion.

[16 marks]

Determinism is a belief that suggests that all behaviours and choices are influenced by internal/external forces that are beyond the control of an individual. There are, however, numerous divisions in relation to what force exactly determines behaviours. One view put forward by B.F. Skinner was that of environmental determinism. Skinner and other behaviourists would suggest that any semblance of free will is actually just a well-founded illusion, as all choices are simply the product of previous experiences of reinforcements or punishments – be this positive or negative – as well as the influence of agents of socialization. Dancho's choice of not quitting and continuing as a famous musician could easily be explained in terms of environmental determinism, as it is likely that the positive reinforcement he gets from 'hearing applause in the concert hall' played a significant part in his decision. Dancho's initial choice of becoming a pianist could also be traced back to the influence of his father as an agent of socialization, as it was he who sent Dancho to a 'specialist music school.'

A benefit that may arise as a result of accepting such beliefs of environmental determinism, and determinism in more general terms, is that it holds merits for the position of Psychology as a subject. The view that all behaviours have a cause – such as those lying in learning events of the past – strongly parallels the emphasis that is put on causal explanations seen in the natural sciences, and in consideration of this, embracing the determinist approach may put Psychology on equal footing with other well-established scientific disciplines, thus contributing to the development of the subject. Although the degree to which determinism can be considered scientific has been strongly debated – with philosophers such as Karl Popper claiming it to be unscientific, given how the notion of causes of behaviour always existing is unfalsifiable in its essence – the belief still contributes to the development of psychology as a science nonetheless, ultimately giving it greater credibility.

Another belief that lies in the determinist approach is that of biological determinism, and this is the view that all behaviours have been influenced by internal biological constructs that cannot be changed through regular means. As such, it is evidently a much harder determinist stance than environmental determinism, as the latter at least allows scope for change via behavioural therapies. Proponents of this belief may explain Dancho's aptitude for piano in terms of genetics – with him being skilled at playing the instrument due to the fact that 'his father was also a concert pianist' – thus leading to the logical conclusion that musical talent and this behaviour seen in Dancho simply runs in his family.

A particular benefit of this strand of the determinist approach is that it may allow treatments for mental disorders to be developed. By acknowledging that conditions, or at least symptoms of these conditions, can be caused by biological factors, this knowledge has fostered the development of psychotherapeutic drug treatments, because pharmaceutical scientists have been able to target the supposed root of these various conditions to tackle them altogether. This suggests that biological determinism specifically holds merits in allowing for outcomes that could improve the quality of life for individuals in such respects – and this ultimately strengthens the credibility of this approach even further.

A final type of determinism is psychic determinism, which is the belief that behaviour is caused by unconscious conflicts that we can't control, as a result of childhood experiences and innate drives (id, ego, and superego). For example, the Psychodynamic Approach suggests that gender behaviours are acquired during the phallic stage of development, through the resolution of the Oedipus/Electra complexes, which results in identification with the same-sex parent.

On the contrary, research has discovered that determinism in more general terms could actually be harmful on an individual level. Numerous studies, such as those conducted by Roberts et al., have discovered that individuals with a stronger belief in fatalism were at greater risk of developing depression later on in life. Although this relationship is correlational in essence, and while there certainly could be other variables explaining such findings – as numerous studies have arrived at the same conclusions, the notion that determinism could actually lead to undesirable outcomes for an individual's mental health is indeed reliable. Ultimately, the determinist approach to explaining behaviour is therefore hindered by the fact that it could decrease the quality of life for individuals in other respects.

Essay questions

Q32 Discuss the free-will and determinism debate. Refer to two topics that you have studied in psychology in your answer.   **[16 marks]**

The free-will vs determinism debate revolves around an attempt by the psychological community to establish which of the two concepts has a greater influence on an individual's choices/ behaviours.

Determinism is the view that an individual's behaviour is shaped or controlled by internal or external forces rather than an individual free will. There are several proponents of determinism: biological determinism suggests that our behaviour is caused by internal biological (genetic, hormonal, evolutionary) factors that are outside of our control. For example, the Biological Approach suggests that OCD is genetic in origin and Nestadt el al found people with 1st degree relatives who suffer from OCD are 5 times more likely to also suffer from OCD. Another type is environmental determinism which is the belief that our behaviour is caused by features of our environment through classical and operant conditioning which we cannot control and finally psychic determinism which advocates that our behaviour is caused by unconscious conflicts. For example, the Psychodynamic Approach suggests that gender behaviours are acquired during the phallic stage of development and through the resolution of Oedipus/Electra complexes, which results in identification with the same sex parent. On the other hand, free will advocates that we play an active role and have a choice in how we behave with no external/internal forces controlling our behaviour. Free will is most closely associated with the humanistic approach where Rogers and Maslow claims that humans are free to control their own behaviour and self-determination is necessary to achieve self-actualisation. They believe humans are motivated towards personal growth and will make choices in order to reach a healthy self-development. The scientific position is determinist as it is based on the belief that all events have a cause and through scientific methods can we explain that behaviour by casual factors.

One of these negative aspects associated with the belief of free will is that in recent times, research studies have provided objective proof refuting the concept as a whole. For example, Benjamin Libet and Chun Siong Soon et al had conducted a study whereby participants – who were wired up to a scanning device – had to decide whether to push a button with either their left or right hand. In this study, it was found that brain activity related to this decision was seen on the scanning device up to 10 seconds before participants had reported being consciously aware of the choice. Although there may be methodological issues in such studies – with the potential inaccuracies regarding the participants own judgements of when they had made the decision exactly – the research still holds significance in demonstrating how free will as a concept lacks validity. Conversely, it also validates the concept of determinism – ultimately providing a case to reject the approach of free will, and to accept that of determinism.

Despite this, other studies have also highlighted the other benefits that may be experienced on an individual level, if the approach is widely accepted. Research has suggested that people with an internal locus of control – in believing that they are essentially the masters of their own destiny – are more likely to be happy than those with a belief in determinism. Roberts et al for example, found that those with a stronger belief in determinism were at a greater risk of developing depression – and this illustrates how believing in free will could well improve the quality of life for individuals. While it must be considered that these conclusions are only correlational in essence – the fact that the relationship has been established on various occasions make the conclusions reliable – and this ultimately provides a greater case to accept the approach of free will, and to reject that of determinism.

However, determinism may also have benefits on an individual level in other respects that free will may not be able to offer – as biological determinism may offer the opportunity for the development of treatments for mental disorders. By acknowledging that conditions, or at least symptoms of these conditions, can be caused by biological factors, this knowledge has fostered the development of psychotherapeutic drug treatments, because pharmaceutical scientists have been able to target the supposed root of these various conditions as to tackle them altogether. A belief in free will does not offer much scope for the development of treatments in such regards – and while it must be acknowledged that other means to tackle mental disorders have still been founded on the premise of free will, such as client-centred therapies for example – this argument still suggests that determinism holds merits in allowing for outcomes that could improve the quality of life for individuals. This strengthens the credibility of the determinism approach, and furthers the case to accept it as a belief over free will.

Moreover, the applicability of determinism in criminal justice system casts doubt over its validity and may point to free will as having more practical application. There have been attempts, in criminal cases in the US for murderers to claim that their behaviour was determined by inherited aggressive tendencies and therefore should not be punished with the death penalty. Stephen Mobley, who killed a pizza shop manager in 1991, claimed this happened because he was 'born to kill' as evidenced by his family history of violence. This argument was rejected and he was sentenced to death. This may suggest that in practice, a determinist position, may be undesirable because it would allow individuals to 'excuse' their behaviour. This could perhaps suggest that within criminal justice systems, the notion of free will may be more helpful.

The nature v nurture debate

Key terms

Q33 Explain the nature v nurture debate in psychology. **[3 marks]**

The nature vs nurture debate is concerned with the extent to which human behaviour are the product of nature or nurture and the relative contribution of each of these influences. Nativists (nature) claim human behaviour is mainly determined by inherited characteristics and genetic/ biological factors. Empiricists (nurture) claim that behaviour is mainly learnt through our experiences that arise from our physical and social environment.

Q34 Explain what is meant by the term 'heredity' in determining behaviour. **[2 marks]**

The term 'heredity' is the process in which certain genes are passed down from parents to their offspring which are expressed to form a characteristic (phenotype).

Q35 Explain what is meant by the term 'environment' in determining behaviour. **[2 marks]**

The term environment refers to any influence on behaviour that is not genetic. It includes matters such as culture that may play a role in determining behaviour.

Q36 Using an example, explain what is meant by an interactional approach in the nature v nurture debate. **[3 marks]**

The interactionist approach is underpinned by the idea that nature and nurture are so intertwined to the extent that they cannot be separated and that separating them can be misleading and lead to an oversimplification. When studying behaviour, the interactionist approach instead involves a consideration of how nature and nurture interact with each other, and an example could be seen through the use of the diathesis stress model, in explaining the development of schizophrenia, where it is caused by a genetic vulnerability that presents itself only when an environmental trigger is activated.

Applications questions

Essay questions

Q37 Discuss the nature-nurture debate. Refer to two topics you have studied in psychology in your answer. **[16 marks]**

The nature vs. nurture debate revolves around the extent to which human behaviour is influenced by innate characteristics (nature) or environmental factors (nurture), as well as the relative contributions of each of these influences. Nativists, who fall under the nature perspective, assert that human behaviour is primarily determined by inherited traits and genetic or biological factors. Empiricists, on the other hand, align with the nurture perspective and argue that behaviour is predominantly learned through experiences shaped by our physical and social surroundings.

Nativists propose that behaviour results from innate biological or genetic factors. Certain characteristics, like eye color and susceptibility to diseases, are deemed biologically determined. Additionally, traits such as height, weight, and hair loss exhibit a positive correlation with genetic relatedness. Characteristics not observed at birth but that emerge later are attributed to maturation—a biological clock that regulates behaviours in a predetermined manner. For instance, research on schizophrenia provides evidence for the nature perspective, as it indicates a higher likelihood of individuals developing the disorder when they share closer genetic relatedness. Gottesman and Shields' 40-family study, for instance, revealed that the risk of schizophrenia increased to 46% when both parents had the disorder. Another study by Gottesman and Shields found a concordance rate of 58% among identical twins.

Empiricists contend that the mind starts as a 'tabula rasa,' a blank slate where experiences fill in the 'blank,' and behaviour and knowledge are products of environmental influences. These environmental factors encompass prenatal experiences, such as the physical and psychological state during pregnancy, as well as postnatal experiences, which encompass social conditions. Research into aggression aligns with the nurture perspective. Bandura et al. conducted experiments involving children exposed to aggressive behaviour exhibited by an adult model on a plastic inflatable bobo doll. The children were then tested for imitative learning, with those in the aggressive condition reproducing aggressive behaviour towards the doll. In contrast, children in the non-aggressive and control groups displayed no aggression. These findings suggest that children are more likely to imitate aggressive behaviour, emphasizing the role of nurture over nature.

The interactionist approach posits that nature and nurture are so intertwined that separating them can be misleading and overly simplistic. Instead of isolating these influences, the interactionist approach considers how they interact with each other. An example of this approach is the diathesis-stress model, which explains the development of schizophrenia as a result of genetic vulnerability triggered by environmental factors. Tienari et al. identified a group of Finnish adoptees, among whom those most likely to develop schizophrenia had biological relatives with a history of the disorder and experienced dysfunctional relationships.

The nurture perspective often implies a deterministic view of behaviour, which can raise ethical concerns. This view suggests that our inherited genetic makeup determines our behaviour, leaving little room for environmental input since it cannot be altered. Ethical implications, such as racism and disparities in opportunities and quality of life, can result from attempts to link genetics with traits like intelligence. For instance, Shockley's claim that genetic factors may contribute to lower IQ scores among Black individuals in the United States sparked controversy.

Conversely, the nurture perspective also carries ethical implications. It proposes that behaviour can be socially engineered by altering environmental conditions. For instance, behaviour shaping and modification are used in therapy to reinforce desirable behaviours and discourage undesirable ones. However, manipulating behaviour, such as suggesting to a CEO to unfairly reward employees working overtime, can be viewed as unethical.

Moreover, it is suggested that aggression may not solely result from environmental influence. Studies like Bandura's bobo doll experiment consistently show that men tend to be more aggressive than women, possibly indicating a genetic explanation. Research by Kalat indicates that sex hormones like testosterone are associated with increased aggression, with higher testosterone levels in men potentially explaining their greater aggression. This suggests that if aggression has a genetic basis rather than being solely influenced by nurture, drug therapies might offer effective prevention strategies.

While research indicates that genetic relatedness increases the risk of developing schizophrenia, it does not necessarily establish a genetic basis for the disorder. Monozygotic twin studies demonstrate that the risk remains below 50% even when individuals share the same genes. This suggests that individual differences result in distinct life experiences, and even monozygotic twins reared together do not exhibit perfect concordance rates. These findings support the idea that heredity and environment cannot be meaningfully separated, making the interactionist approach a more comprehensive explanation for human behaviour.

Holism and reductionism

Key terms

Q38 Explain the holism and reductionism debate in psychology. **[3 marks]**

Reductionism is concerned with breaking down a complex phenomenon into simpler components, making it more desirable for a simpler level of explanation. However, holism is an approach that perceives the whole experience rather than focusing on individual features or their relations. This debate revolves around the extent to which behaviour can be explained through reductionism or holism.

Q39 Explain what is meant by 'holism'. **[3 marks]**

Holism is an approach that, concerning behaviour, perceives the entire experience rather than just individual features or their interactions. Holism is most closely associated with humanistic psychology, which believes that individuals should be seen as unique wholes rather than mere collections of stimulus-response links.

Q40 Explain what is meant by 'reductionism'. **[3 marks]**

Reductionism is the practice of understanding behaviours by breaking them down into their smaller constituent parts. It follows the philosophy of Occam's Razor and involves using various levels of explanation to understand a given behaviour. For instance, biological reductionism assumes that we are biological organisms composed of physiological structures and processes, suggesting that all behaviour can be explained through biological influences.

Q41 Using an example, explain what is meant by levels of explanation in psychology. **[4 marks]**

The use of 'Levels of explanation' is a tool employed to understand behaviours, suggesting that there are various ways to view a given phenomenon, with some being more reductionist than others. For example, consider OCD, which can be understood at the socio-cultural level, the most holistic, as a condition involving irrational actions. At a psychological level, it can be seen as the experience of having obsessive thoughts. More reductionist explanations might attribute OCD to the hypersensitivity of the basal ganglia (physiological) or an underproduction of OCD (neurochemical explanation, the most reductionistic).

Q42 Using an example of a topic, you have studied in psychology, distinguish between biological and reductionism and environmental reductionism. **[5 marks]**

Biological reductionism is based on the premise that we are biological organisms composed of physiological structures and processes, explaining behaviour through neurochemical, physiological, and genetic influences. For instance, the biological dopamine hypothesis explains schizophrenia with excessive dopamine levels in the subcortex, leading to antipsychotic treatments like chlorpromazine. In contrast, environmental reductionism posits that all observable behaviour can be explained through stimulus-response links, often linked to past experiences. For schizophrenia, this might involve environmental triggers like childhood family dysfunction, associated with increased schizophrenia risk in adulthood.

Q43 Briefly give one strength of taking a reductionist approach in psychology. **[3 marks]**

A strength of adopting a reductionist approach in studying behaviour is that it helps psychologists identify the most influential level of explanation. This is particularly significant in conditions like mental disorders, where it may enable pharmaceutical scientists to develop more targeted treatments. Thus, reductionism offers practical advantages that can enhance people's quality of life.

Q44 Briefly give one limitation of taking a reductionist approach in psychology. **[3 marks]**

A weakness of the reductionist approach is that focusing solely on lower levels of explanation may overlook the meaning behind behaviour. This oversight can lead to fundamental errors in understanding. For instance, Wolpe (1973) treated a woman for a fear of insects with systematic desensitization but found no improvement. Later, he discovered that her husband had an insect-related nickname. Her fear was not due to classical conditioning but was a representation of marital problems. Concentrating solely on the behavioural level and ignoring the underlying meaning would have been an error. The danger of lower levels of explanation is that they may divert attention from a more appropriate level of explanation.

Applications questions

Essay questions

Q45 Discuss the holism and reductionism debate. Refer to one topic you have studied in psychology in your answer. **[16 marks]**

Reductionism involves breaking down a complex phenomenon into simpler components, and advocates of reductionism argue that this process is desirable because behaviours are best understood in terms of a simpler explanation. Within reductionism, there are different levels of explanations employed to understand a behaviour, with some explanations more reductionist than others. For example, OCD can be explained in various ways: socio-culturally, as producing behaviour that is regarded as odd/irrational; psychologically, as the experience of having obsessive thoughts; physiologically, through the hypersensitivity of the basal ganglia; neurochemically – the underproduction of serotonin. One example is biological reductionism, which is based on the premise that we are biological organisms made up of physiological structures and processes. Thus, all our behaviour can be reduced to a neurochemical, physiological, or genetic influence. For example, the dopamine hypothesis states that there are excessive levels of dopamine in the subcortex, which has led to the development of antipsychotics such as chlorpromazine, which has been effective in managing schizophrenic symptoms. Another example is environmental reductionism, which is based on the premise that all observable behaviour can be explained through a stimulus-response link, and this can be seen through the explanation of phobias by classical and operant conditioning in acquiring and maintaining the phobia.

Holism, on the other hand, doesn't involve any notion of breaking a behaviour down, but rather perceives the whole experience rather than the individual factors and/or the relations between them. Holism is most closely related to humanistic psychology, who believe that the individual should be seen as unique and taken as a whole rather than a set of stimulus-response links – what matters most is a sense of unified identity, and a lack of this can lead to mental disorders.

A weakness of the reductionist explanation is that while the lower levels are indeed a part of any account of behaviour, if these lower levels (e.g., biological/behavioural explanations) are taken in isolation, then the meaning of the behaviour may be overlooked. This may then lead to fundamental errors of understanding. For example, Wolpe (1973), who developed the therapy for systematic desensitization, treated one woman for a fear of insects. He found no improvement from this behavioural method, but he later found out her husband had an insect nickname, so her fear was not as a result of classical conditioning but a means of representing her marital problems; to focus on the behavioural level alone and ignore the meaning would have been an error. The danger of lower levels of explanations is that they may distract us from a more appropriate level.

Moreover, while reducing behaviour to a lower, more observable level that can be studied is productive and necessary to improve our understanding, experimental research has produced an array of findings about human behaviour, and thus there are questions raised about how applicable reductionist explanations are to everyday life. For example, the findings from lab experiments, researching eyewitness testimony, such as Loftus and Palmer, have not always been confirmed by studies of real-life eyewitnesses, where memories have been found to be highly inaccurate. The operationalization of variables in eyewitness testimony may be measurable, but it bears no similarity to studies in real life. One reason this may be is due to the effect of anxiety and shock on our memories, which can affect how much we remember. Therefore, findings from experiments may not reflect real life, and thus reductionist explanations may not be of practical value in our lives.

On the other hand, holism may have a greater application to everyday life, as often there are aspects of social behaviour that only emerge within a group context and can't be understood at the level of the individual group members. For instance, the effects of conformity to social roles and the deindividuation of the prisoners and guards in the Stanford Prison Experiment could not be understood by studying the participants as individuals; it was the interaction between people and the behaviour of the group that was important. However, holistic explanations in psychology tend not to lend themselves to scientific testing and can become vague and speculative as they become more complex. For example, humanistic psychology tends to be criticized for its lack of empirical evidence and is instead seen by many as a rather 'loose set of concepts.' Moreover, higher-level explanations, which combine perspectives present researchers with a practical dilemma: if we accept that there are many factors that contribute to depression, it becomes difficult to establish the most influential and which one to use as a treatment option. This suggests that when it comes to finding solutions for real-life problems, lower, more reductionist explanations may be more appropriate.

One alternative to reductionism, which is subtly different from holism, is the interactionist stance. Whereas holism is more concerned with higher-level explanations of behaviour, such as the behaviour of individuals within a group, interactionism considers how different levels of explanation may combine and interact. An example of the interactionist approach is the diathesis-stress model which has been used to explain the onset of schizophrenia. It suggests that early psychological trauma like child abuse has the ability to seriously affect many aspects of brain development. For example, it could cause the HPA system to be overactive, making the person much more vulnerable to later stress which can lead to schizophrenia. This model has led to a more multidisciplinary and 'holistic' approach to treatment – combining drugs and family therapy.

Q46 'Psychologists sometimes adopt a reductionist approach to their investigations when they want their research to be objective and empirical.'

Discuss reductionism in psychological research. Refer to the statement above in your answer.

[16 marks]

Reductionism involves breaking down complex phenomena into simpler components. Advocates of reductionism argue that this process is desirable because behaviours are best understood with simpler explanations. Within reductionism, different levels of explanation are employed to understand behaviour, with some being more reductionist than others. For example, OCD can be explained in various ways: socio-culturally, as producing behaviour regarded as odd/irrational; psychologically, as the experience of having obsessive thoughts; physiologically, through the hypersensitivity of the basal ganglia; neurochemically, involving the underproduction of serotonin. One example is biological reductionism, which is based on the premise that we are biological organisms composed of physiological structures and processes. Thus, all our behaviour can be reduced to neurochemical, physiological, or genetic influences. For example, the dopamine hypothesis posits excessive levels of dopamine in the subcortex, leading to the development of antipsychotics like chlorpromazine, effective in managing schizophrenic symptoms. Another example is environmental reductionism, which assumes that all observable behaviour can be explained through stimulus-response links, as seen in the explanation of phobias through classical and operant conditioning.

The scientific method states that evidence should be observable and unaffected by subjective interpretation, and the best way to achieve this is to adopt a reductionist approach because it leads to research being objective and empirical. For instance, biopsychologists use experimental research methods within biological reductionism to study physiological processes. They can objectively measure chemical brain activity using MRI and EEG to observe the effects of drugs on neurotransmitters, measuring changes in behaviour. Furthermore, environmental reductionism allows the testing of stimulus-response links, such as classical and operant conditioning, through the manipulation of stimuli presented systematically and the objective recording of responses involving only observable behaviour – empiricism.

A weakness of the reductionist explanation is that while lower levels are indeed part of any account of behaviour, taking these lower levels, such as biological or behavioural explanations, in isolation may overlook the meaning of the behaviour, leading to fundamental errors of understanding. For example, Wolpe (1973), who developed systematic desensitization therapy, treated a woman for a fear of insects. He found no improvement from this behavioural method, but later discovered that her husband had an insect nickname. Her fear was not a result of classical conditioning but a means of representing her marital problems. Focusing solely on the behavioural level and ignoring the meaning would have been an error. The danger of lower levels of explanation is that they may distract us from a more appropriate level.

While reducing behaviour to a lower, more observable level for study is productive and necessary to improve our understanding, experimental research has produced an array of findings about human behaviour. Thus, questions are raised about how applicable reductionist explanations are to everyday life. For example, findings from lab experiments on eyewitness testimony, such as Loftus and Palmer's, have not always been confirmed by studies of real-life eyewitnesses, where memories have been found to be highly inaccurate. The operationalization of variables in eyewitness testimony may be measurable but bears no similarity to real-life studies. One reason for this may be the effect of anxiety and shock on our memories, which can influence how much we remember. Therefore, findings from experiments may not reflect real life, and reductionist explanations may not be practically valuable in our lives.

Idiographic and nomothetic

Key term

Q47 Which of the following best describes an idiographic approach in psychology?　　**[1 mark]**

Shade **one** box only.

- A. Studying individuals in order to establish general laws of behaviour.
- B. Studying individuals without intending to establish general laws of behaviour.
- C. Studying large samples in order to establish general laws of behaviour.
- D. Studying large samples without intending to establish general laws of behaviour.

Q48 Which of the following statements best describes a nomothetic approach in psychology?
[1 mark]

Shade **one** box only.

Psychologists taking a nomothetic approach...

- A. study single cases and do not formulate general laws.
- B. study groups of people and do not formulate general laws
- C. study groups of people and formulate general laws.
- D. study single cases and formulate general laws.

Q49 Explain one strength of the idiographic approach.　　**[3 marks]**

One strength of the idiographic approach is that it strongly compliments the nomothetic approach. By using methods such as case studies alongside general principles, the approach to psychology has the potential to prove, deepen, or even refute these existing laws. Ultimately, the approach therefore holds value in allowing the psychological community to deepen their understanding on various behaviours

Q50 Explain one limitation of the idiographic approach in psychology.　　**[3 marks]**

A limitation of the idiographic approach is that research from such methods tends to be restricted in nature. This is because means associated with idiographic research, such as case studies, offer findings which cannot be generalised to the wider population – due to the fact that it does not provide an adequate baseline to which behaviour can be compared. By not offering general understandings of human behaviour, idiographic research is therefore limited in its application

Q51 Explain two differences between idiographic and nomothetic approach to psychological investigations. **[2 marks + 2 marks]**

The idiographic approach aims to study the subjective experiences of an individual, in order to develop a detailed account of their behaviours, while the nomothetic approach on the other hand aims to study the experiences of large numbers of people, in order to develop a general understanding of behaviours through laws/principles. Another difference is that the idiographic approach tends to employ more qualitative methods of research such as by case studies, while the nomothetic approach usually utilises the quantitative methods such as lab experiments.

Application questions

Q52 Read the item and then answer the question that follows.

> A prison psychologist used an idiographic approach to study offending. He asked two offenders to record their thoughts about their childhood and their offending behaviour in a journal over a period of four weeks.
>
> Qualitative analysis of the journals showed that the offenders often thought about sad childhood events and believed that their childhood experiences had influenced their offending.
>
> Findings from idiographic research like the study described above are often used as a basis for other investigations.

Explain how the researcher might develop the above investigation through taking a nomothetic approach. **[6 marks]**

As findings from such idiographic research are 'used as a basis for other investigations', the researcher could develop the above investigation into taking more of a nomothetic approach. This would first involve the formulation of a testable hypothesis – such as a directional one stating that violent offenders would have more negative thoughts about their childhood than non-violent ones. The researcher should also employ standardised conditions e.g. ask the offenders to record their thoughts at the same time of day. As nomothetic research involves the data collection from a large sample, they should ask a larger number of offenders to record their thoughts (over 20 offenders). They should employ techniques such as stratified sampling to this end, as to ensure that any final conclusions could be generalised to the target population. Any findings would then be analysed by means such as statistical testing, as to ultimately establish a general law/principle regarding the relationship between past experiences and how this may lead to offending.

Essay questions

Discuss idiographic and/or nomothetic approaches to psychological investigation. **[16 marks]**

The idiographic approach in psychology seeks to describe the unique nature of individuals, treating them as distinct entities with their own subjective experiences, motivations, and values. It typically employs qualitative research methods like case studies, unstructured interviews, and self-report measures. The central goal is to capture the richness of the human experience and gain insights into an individual's perspective. Humanistic psychology aligns closely with idiography and takes a phenomenological approach to studying human beings, focusing on the whole person.

One strength of the idiographic approach lies in its use of in-depth qualitative methods, which provide a comprehensive and holistic account of an individual. Moreover, the detailed nature of idiography can complement or challenge general principles. For instance, the experimental research involving HM conducted by Corkin demonstrated his ability to form long-term procedural memories for simple motor skills. HM's case has been invaluable in revealing how different types of long-term memory are more resistant to forgetting and may be stored in different brain areas. This strength lies in the ability of a single case to generate further hypotheses and offer important insights into normal functioning, thereby enhancing our understanding.

However, a limitation of the idiographic approach is its perceived lack of scientific rigor. This concern has contributed to the rise of positive psychology, which argues that humanistic psychology, associated with idiography, lacks sufficient empirical evidence, potentially rendering its findings meaningless. For example, the development of the Oedipus complex was primarily based on a single case study, which is susceptible to bias and tends to lack scientific rigor, making it difficult to draw meaningful generalizations without a comparative baseline. Qualitative methods propose a solution by advocating reflexivity, where researchers critically reflect on factors affecting participant behaviour during the research process. Removing these factors could render qualitative research more scientific.

The nomothetic approach in psychology involves studying large groups of people to establish general laws or principles of behaviour. Laboratory studies are often associated with nomothetic research. An example of this approach is the behaviourist perspective in psychology, which extensively studied numerous rats, cats, and pigeons to develop laws of learning.

A limitation of the nomothetic approach is that it can diminish individuality. The quest for general laws and predictions may lead to the neglect of the whole person within psychology. For instance, in memory laboratory studies, participants are treated as mere sets of scores, disregarding their individuality and subjective experiences in the situation. This weakness suggests that while seeking generalizations, the nomothetic approach might sometimes overlook the richness of human experiences.

On the other hand, one strength of the nomothetic approach is its strong scientific foundation. This approach employs research methods, such as laboratory studies, commonly used in the natural sciences. It includes testing under standardized conditions, using data sets, and employing statistical analyses, as seen in IQ testing. These processes have allowed psychologists to establish norms for typical behaviour, enhancing the scientific credibility of the field of psychology.

Ethical implications

Key terms

Q54   Explain what is meant by ethical implications.   **[3 marks]**

Ethical implications refer to the wider ramifications that may be observed after conducting a study, particularly one of a socially sensitive nature. These implications can include the impact on shaping society's views of a particular group, such as reinforcing prejudices, or influencing social policies. For instance, in Milgram's research study, participants experienced significant distress throughout the experiment and were unable to provide informed consent. However, they were later debriefed and underwent follow-up interviews, revealing no signs of long-term psychological effects. While this had ethical implications for the participants, it contributed to our understanding of societal behaviour regarding obedience.

Q55   Outline one ethical implication of psychological research.   **[3 marks]**

One ethical implication of psychological research is the potential influence of study findings on shaping government social policies. If a study suggests the need for new legislations for the greater good, governments may introduce new laws accordingly. For instance, Bowlby's Maternal Deprivation Theory, which emphasized the importance of the mother-infant relationship, influenced custody laws by insinuating that fathers may not be as suitable in custody battles.

Q56   Explain what is meant by 'socially sensitive' research.   **[3 marks]**

'Socially sensitive research' refers to studies that may have broader implications for the participants involved or for the larger societal groups they represent. This term is often associated with studies investigating taboo topics in psychology, such as ethnicity or sexuality. Given the increased attention these topics receive, socially sensitive research carries a higher risk of wider implications. For example, Shockley's suggestion of a genetic basis for low IQ scores in African-Americans sparked debate and could potentially lead to prejudice and discrimination.

Q57   Explain how one example of research could be considered socially sensitive.   **[4 marks]**

'Socially sensitive research' refers to studies that may have broader implications for the participants involved or for the larger societal groups they represent. This term is often associated with studies investigating taboo topics in psychology, such as ethnicity or sexuality. Given the increased attention these topics receive, socially sensitive research carries a higher risk of wider implications.

For example, Shockley's suggestion of a genetic basis for low IQ scores in African-Americans sparked debate and could potentially lead to prejudice and discrimination.Application questions.

Application questions

Q58 Read the item and then answer the questions that follow.

> In a study of antisocial activity and social background, researchers interviewed 100 children aged 14 years. They then classified each child according to their level of antisocial activity. They concluded that 26 were 'very antisocial', 40 were 'mildly antisocial', and 34 were 'not antisocial'. The researchers found that the majority of the 'very antisocial' children attended Crayford secondary school, whereas most of the other two groups of children attended another local school.

The study on the opposite page is an example of socially sensitive research.

Q59 Briefly explain how the researchers could have dealt with the issue of social sensitivity in this study.   **[4 marks]**

One socially sensitive aspect of the research above is the implications of the study's findings on Crayford Secondary School, in that it may be viewed by society as being an establishment that fosters anti-social activity. Another potential concern is how society might perceive the children from the researched area in a negative manner. To address these issues, researchers should ensure that the specific school is not identified when publishing their findings.

Essay question

Q60 Discuss one or more ethical implications of research in psychology. Refer to at least one topic you have studied in psychology in your answer.   **[16 marks]**

Ethical implications consider the impact of psychological research on the rights of individuals in a broader context, particularly on the participants. This extends to societal levels, influencing public policy and perceptions of certain groups.

One ethical implication of research is the effect of publication on the wider public. For instance, Bowlby's research on attachments suggests that it is the most crucial relationship a baby will experience. This has societal implications as it reinforces the idea that women should primarily stay at home to care for children rather than pursue careers. It may also have economic implications. Additionally, it could add unnecessary stress to mothers who may feel guilty about returning to work and placing their infants in childcare. Moreover, it implies that fathers are less important than mothers, potentially impacting custodial battles where fathers are seen as inferior. If Bowlby's findings are incorrect, it could have denied men the opportunity to raise their children.

Another ethical implication concerns the potential use of research findings by the government, leading to changes in legislation. In the 1920s in America, several states passed compulsory sterilization laws based on the influence of the psychological community, targeting individuals deemed "feeble" and "unfit to breed." This had ramifications for specific societal groups, including those with low IQs, drug addicts, and the mentally ill. In the UK, Burt's twin study influenced public policy by showing a concordance rate in intelligence, supporting the notion of genetic intelligence. This led to the development of 11+ exams, resulting in segregation between wealthier and less wealthy students, where those who could afford private tuition were more likely to pass and attend better grammar schools.

Despite the ethical concerns associated with research on controversial and taboo topics, studying underrepresented groups and issues can promote greater sensitivity and understanding. This can help reduce prejudice, encourage acceptance, and foster inclusivity. For instance, research on the unreliability of eyewitness testimony (EWT) has reduced the risk of miscarriages of justice within the legal system, leading to a decreased reliance on witness testimony in court. This is a strength as such research plays a valuable role in improving society.

It might be tempting to suggest that the solution to handling research with ethical implications is to avoid it altogether. For instance, avoiding research on topics like homosexuality, race, gender, and addiction due to potential negative consequences for participants or society (socially sensitive). However, this would leave psychologists with nothing to examine but trivial issues. Sieber and Stanley argue that ignoring sensitive research is an irresponsible approach to science, as psychologists have a duty to conduct such research to benefit society.

Sieber and Stanley (1998) caution that the way research questions are framed and investigated can influence the interpretation of findings, similar to how cross-cultural research may be biased by ethnocentrism, with researchers from different cultures believing in their cultural superiority. Kitzinger and Coyle (1995) found that research on "alternative relationships" exhibited a form of "heterosexual bias," comparing and judging these relationships against heterosexual norms without considering their unique characteristics. This suggests that researchers must approach such research with different preconceptions to avoid misrepresenting minority groups.

Research involving ethical implications may also be compromised when it is used by governments and institutions to shape social policy without full consideration of the environmental factors influencing characteristics like intelligence. Additionally, seemingly harmless research may have socially sensitive consequences. For example, in the 1950s, research on the persuasive effects of subliminal messages was used by marketing companies for advertising purposes. One study claimed that flashing images of Coca-Cola and popcorn on cinema screens significantly increased sales. Many cinemas implemented these images, but it was later discovered that the study's author fabricated the findings. Although the harm in this context was limited, research aimed at manipulating the public raises ethical concerns and questions who benefits from such research.

Answers to identification questions

Cultural bias in Psychology

Q11   C.
            D.

Free-will and determinism

Q18   C.
            E.

Idiographic and nomothetic

Q47   B.

Q48   C.

www.ingramcontent.com/pod-product-compliance
Lightning Source LLC
Chambersburg PA
CBHW081229020426

42333CB00018B/2469